THE REVOLUTIONARY and other poems
STEPHEN MORRIS

Other books by Stephen Morris include:—

Alien Poets (with G. Levine) 1965
Wanted (with Peter Finch) 1968
Doubts & Memories 1969
Penny Farthing Madness 1969 (reprinted 1970 & 1973)
*Born Under Leo 1971
*The Revolutionary 1972 (1st Edn.)
*The Kingfisher Catcher 1974

* Published by Aquila

the revolutionary and other poems

stephen morris

aquila poetry

Acknowledgements are due to the editors of the following publications, in which most of these poems have appeared, or are due to appear:-

Bitterroot (USA); Brushfire (USA); Canadian Sunrise; Contrasts; Express & Star (Wolverhampton); Forge; Gargantua; Imprint; International Times; The Journal; Lines; Lyrismos (USA); Muse; Ma Boheme; Mac; Poetry Workshop; Red Mole; Samphire; Sausalito Belvedere Gazette (USA); Sol; Sub; Tribune; Wen; The Guardian; Coventry Evening Telegraph; Daily Mirror; Birmingham Evening Mail; Wolverhampton Magazine; Nottingham Topic; Nottingham Evening Post; The Observer; Sunday Times; Time Out; Grapevine; Times Higher Education Supplement.

2nd (revised & enlarged) edition. First published in 1975 by Aquila. First edition published in 1972, in paperback, casebound, and ltd signed cased editions, both cased editions still available. This edition published in paperback only.

ISBN 0 903226 33 2

Published by:—
The Aquila Publishing Company Ltd., Isle of Skye, Scotland.
Distributed by:—
Aquila/IBD, 11 Novi Lane, Leek, Staffs. ST13 6NS.

CONTENTS

for JOHN SWEET

LATE ONE NIGHT

I was woken up very late one night
By the sound of a heart gently breaking
Inside the sleeping body of my wife.
She lay in her innocence in trust,
Listened to my twisted, miserable lies,
Smiled sadly, as if wanting to believe,
Then turned and went unhappily to sleep.
We had lain together, very much apart,
Her back curved towards me, so I'd kissed her,
As if to apologise for my sins,
But it was wasted and of no avail;
For I was woken very late one night
By the sound of a heart gently breaking
Inside the sleeping body of my wife.

FALLING TEARS

The holly tree sits at Christmas
It's breast speckled over in blood
The snow falls gently around it
As white feathers in a field of love.
The air is as soft as chiffon
Whispering amens and praise,
And there burns a terrible fire
Where humans die in pain.
From out of a pit of hate
Tired eyes peer up in despair,
Where men plead for understanding
And mutter forgotten prayers.
The children play on in the garden
The lovers wait for peace,
The soldiers have lost their battle,
The tears roll down, then cease.

POLITICAL POEM

NI⚡ON

WI£SON

JOHN$ON

KE◇◇EDY

INVASION

They had taken over;
The ignorance of ourselves
Was now complete.
Pieces of iron
Were entering
The flesh of the living,
Children cried in fear,
The old, tired of life, died.
They had taken over;
Their silence told lies,
Their actions were truth.
In my clenched fist
I carried a thousand promises,
But they had taken over
Leaving only lost dreams and fear.

sex poem

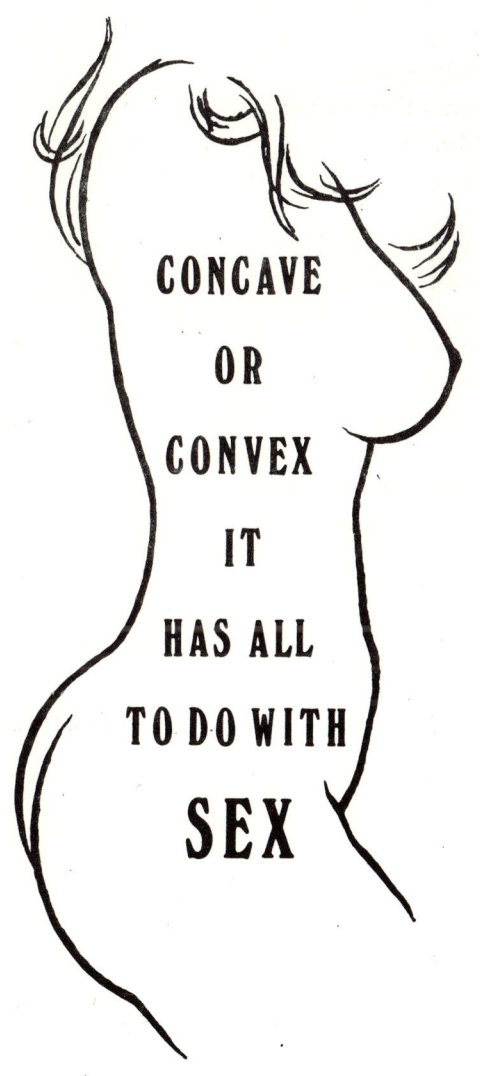

CONCAVE
OR
CONVEX
IT
HAS ALL
TO DO WITH
SEX

CAN THIS BE SERIOUS?

Galloping horses
A running stream
Freudian symbolism
My wet dream

Phallic symbols
Mammary glands
A curved breast
My penis stands

A Rorschach test
A killer's knife
Sexual intercourse
My mother's wife

Am I subnormal
Am I a genius
An I.Q. Test
Can this be serious?

Old Star Movie Poem

CHAPLIN

♡alentino

JOLSON

Garb

BRIEF POEM

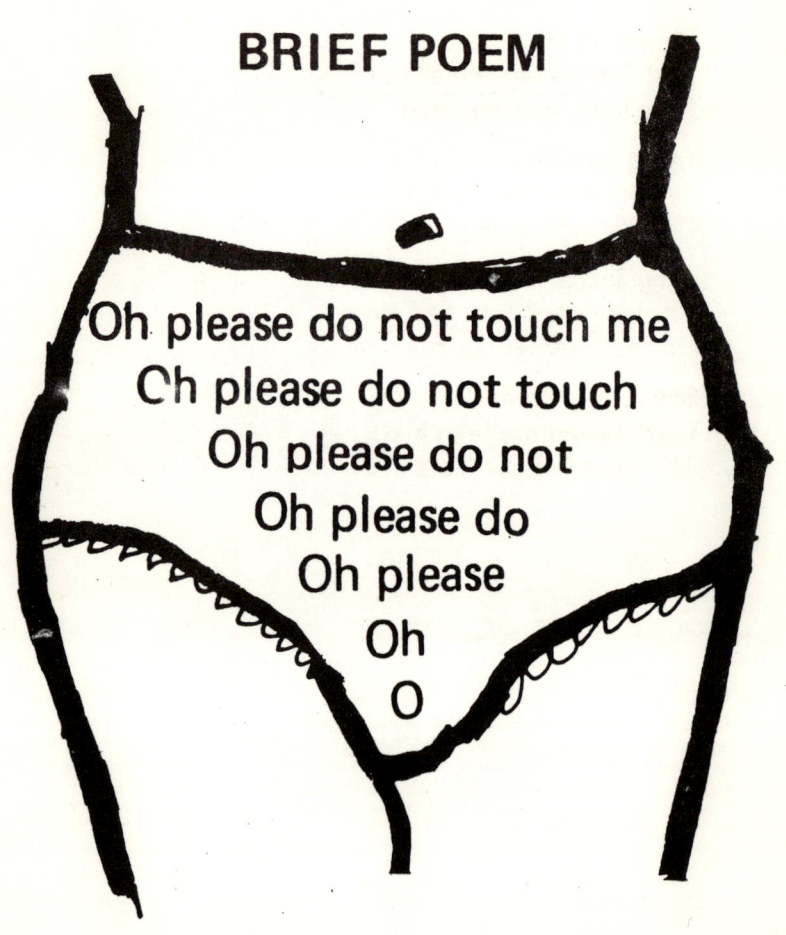

Oh please do not touch me
Oh please do not touch
Oh please do not
Oh please do
Oh please
Oh
O

LOVE STORY HAIKU

We met in the Spring
And flowers blossomed our love.
Love lasts, we whispered.

Lying together,
Sunkissed on hot sand, kissing,
Holding each other.

When leaves gently fell,
The long days drew to a close,
Our ways moved apart.

She died in Winter
Carrying our unborn child.
The snow fell like tears.

YOU STAND

You stand
Like a gazelle
Or a white mare
Drinking water
From a blue pool.
You stand
Like a lost rabbit
Or as you are –
A young girl
Waiting hopefully
For a late lover.
You stand
Like a black cat
At midnight
Green-eyed.
You stand
Like a lonely rose
Swelling your beauty,
Or a lost child
Bewildered.
You stand,
You stand waiting,
Waiting for me.

french poem

FLIRTATION

An empty envelope
Without an address
An empty wine glass
Marked with lipstick,
Two hands' fingertips touching.
Two lips waiting
Whispering wishes
Waiting for wishbones
To wish our love would last,
Or perhaps merely begin.
Your blue-grey eyes twinkled,
Responding to my flirtation,
And your lips parted
As if waiting for my kiss.
But you pause slightly
As if my image
Had clouded something
Very precious,
Leaving me feeling
As an empty envelope
Without an address,
Or an empty wine glass
Marked with lipstick.

GOLDEN RINGS

Your fingers were rich with rings,
Placed upon them in golden moments
By a lonely man who sits
In your home minding a sleeping child,
Waiting for your late return.
Those same fingers which beckoned to me,
Touching me, until I wanted you,
Guided me through passion to shame.
Occasionally I think of the sleeping child
Who has no rings to mark his love,
Nor goodnight kisses from mother or lover,
But who has a father who sits and waits
Knowing the agony of unfaithful gold.

FLY POEM

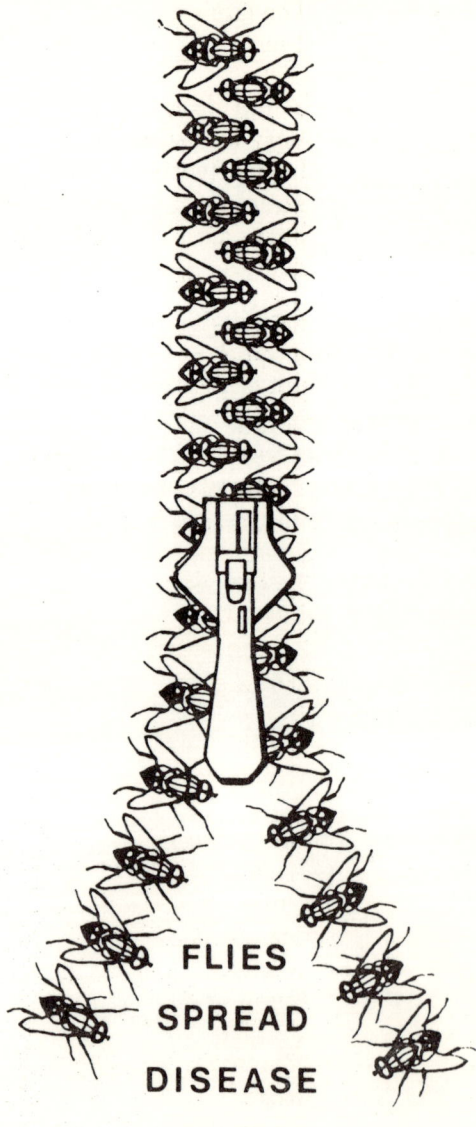

FLIES
SPREAD
DISEASE

KEEP YOURS DONE UP

FOR THE BEST

The late -
Teened
Girl
Young dark
Very beautiful
Inadvertently
Took
From me
A male
Seed
Which grew
Within
Her and
Within
A year
To eight
Pounds
No ounces
To introduce
Himself
To the world
With
A cry
Causing pain
Which was
Soon
Forgotten
In smiles
Until
The Social
Worker
Came
To take
The boy
Away
To responsibility
In marriage
But it was
For the best
So they said

TR**O**SKY

C**A**PONE

MAN UNI**T**ED

THE MORNING PAPER

Read *The Guardian*
Drank my tea,
Why wouldn't she
Look at me?

Read of the Irish
I should care,
It's the Revolution
I should be there.

In my mind
I fought in Spain,
Fought in Bolivia
Died in vain.

Should buy *The Star*
Should read *The Mole*,
One million workers
On the dole.

Went to Villa Park
Saw my team,
The Second Division
Where've they been?

Ate Indian curry
Drank China tea,
South African oranges
Remember me?

Jack-boots marching
Shirts need starching,
Bodies lying
In pits of lime.

Concentration camps
Anglepoise lamps,
"H" bombs falling
Who's that calling?

Listened to the news
We're all repressed,
I've read *The Guardian*
I'm so depressed.

FLAG POEM

UK

USA

USSR

FRANCE

THE MOURNERS

The funeral marched around
My body.
The mourners
Were weeping
For the silent dead.
They stamped, they halted,
They turned around,
They walked with legs
And feet of lead.
They had diamonds
Laced along their sleeves
And money was sprinkled
Around their minds.
There were clocks upon
Their timeless faces
And they were cloaked
With the indifference
Of unchecked time.
Suddenly a wave of love
Seeped through
Their sunkissed skins
When the midnight
Sun eclipsed,
Leaving the mourners
With lunatic grins.
At daybreak they were all gone,
The funeral over, the morning sun.

OUR FIRST KISS

Slipping down
To the edge of the sky
The sun sets.
Like an enormous
Red balloon
Bringing the day
To an end
The flowers fold
Themselves
And bow their heads
Swaying gently
In the soft wind
As if to acknowledge
The black blanket
Of night
Suddenly you turn
To me and the cool
Moonlight falls
Resting and reflecting
Your warm eyes
And your moist lips
Which part slightly
Suggesting our first kiss
We pause to rest
Our bodies nervously
Against one another
Then the sun explodes
And the flowers awake
With joy.

FRENCHMAN

ITALIAN

SPIARD

GERMAN

VAN GOGH

LICHTENSTEIN

RENOIR

MODIGLIANI

THE OLD MEN IN THE PARK

The old men in the park
Sit gazing blankly back
To their first world war
They watch the falling leaves
Which remind them of fallen comrades
Their white hairs like white feathers
Mark their years and their yesterdays
Then the sun dies bringing Autumn twilight

The old men in the park
Listen for the golden bugle
But hear only the dusk bell
Which the keeper rings to close.
One by one the old men
Scuffle away into a new night
Wondering how to face the distant past
But more afraid of the distant future

THE BULLFIGHTER

The bullfighter said his prayers
In the morning, and then again at noon.
He said them yet again at two
And at four he said goodbye.
At five he walked out to the sun,
For today was the day the bullfighter had to die.

The bullfighter faced death at five
In the storm of one black bull.
When his death came there was a sudden still,
The crowd it hushed in wake.
The bull had moved then twisted round,
The fighter had made his last mistake.

The bullfighter died in the hot afternoon,
His twenty years seeped away.
They carried him out in his suit of lights,
They carried him shoulder high.
But he had no ears or tail to show,
For today was the day the bullfighter had to die.

UNTOUCHED

Untouched
Untouchable
For her
Today is tomorrow
Was yesterday
Fingers snapping
Swaying
Body moving
Chasing lost notes
Eyes closed
Twisting
Capturing
The music
Untouched
Her long
Small breasted
Body
Swaying
Untouchable
For her
Today is tomorrow
Was yesterday

numbers poem

1NE
2WO
3HREE
4OUR

CORNFLOWER EYES

Cornflower Eyes
   cornflower eyes
My little girl has
   cornflower eyes
Long brown thighs
   long brown thighs
My little girl has
   long brown thighs
What a surprise
   for cornflower eyes
When I tell her lies
From the bottom to the top
Of her long brown thighs
   cornflower eyes

TEA TIME

The girl with eyes
   as big as shop windows
Looked at me.

The question had been posed.

Yes, I said,
And the tea cups
   rattled their consent.

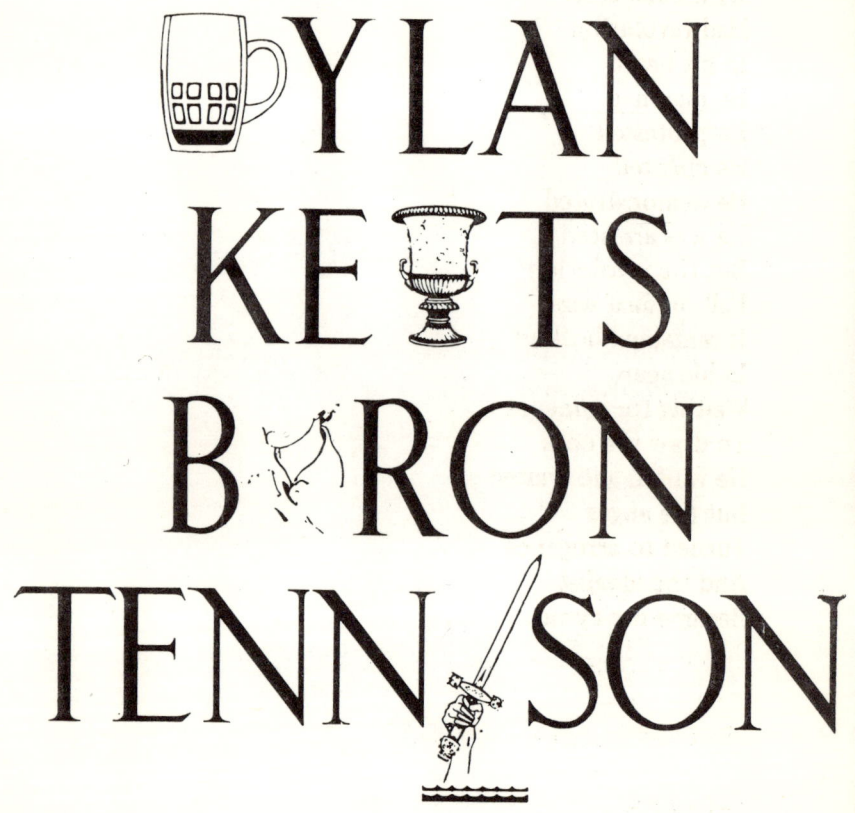

THE REVOLUTIONARY

The young man
With a red scarf
Had revolution
In his heart
He marched
He protested
He chanted
He demonstrated
He was arrested
But the revolution
Fell on deaf ears
It remained bottled
In his heart
Waiting for someone
To draw the cork
He waited and waited
But the anger
Turned to arrogance
And the idealist
Became the cynic.

DRIVING HOME

Driving home,
Through long avenues
Of Winter trees,
Their branches
Stretching upwards
Like arms
Towards
The blue sky.
Driving home,
Past cottages,
Their chimneys
Bursting out
With blue smoke
Which curls
Like question marks
Into the sky.
Driving home,
Thinking of you,
Dreams suddenly
Shattered
Like splintered
Windscreens
Cutting the flesh
In a steering wheel
Of death.
I was driving home,
Driving home,
Driving home
To you.

A HEAVY SCENE

H
E
A
V
Y

The elderly man with grey temples
Who wore   a suit   and carried
A brown brief case to work every-day
Came on a very heavy scene
When I told him about his daughter
And her very strange ways in bed

But what really sent him out of shape
Was when I told him that his wife
Usually joined in the fun as well

THE PAIN OF LOVING

One warm afternoon
My young love, whose eyes
Rained tears after we
First made love, confessed
That she also a
Tutor had become —
To her own young love.

When you first made love
Did he cry as well?
Was my bitter cry.
She did not, was her
Reply. Her eyes rained
Tears, but they were for
Joy, not bloody pain.

spring

SUMMER

autumn

WINTER

THOUGHTS OF LOVE

When the postman
Came that morning
He brought a small
Square packet.
I did not, I remember
Recognise the typewriter
And recalled
That it was
Not my birthday
For more than
Half a year.
Beneath the brown paper,
Bound with sellotape,
I found a small, square
Pink plastic container.
What on earth . . . . was it?
Inside, to my amazement —
A circle of rubber,
Sprinkled with powder.
The note, which lay
Across it, explained all.
"Don't take any chances,
And I hope that this
Will fit my poor replacement."
She'd always been
A thoughtful wife.

THE OLD MAN

The old man sighed,
Then smiled
A while,
And brushed his sleeve,
As if he were tired.
Death, he often said,
Comes in many ways.
It is brought by assassins
To men of high state,
It comes to the man
Who opens the gate.
It comes in the evening
When lovers lie still,
It comes in the morning
When beggars kill.
The old man knew
When he looked to the clouds,
So he brushed his sleeve
And he kissed the flowers.

ONE NIGHT STAND

I met her at a party
I asked her to dance
I knew it was the beginning
Of a brand new romance

It was a one night stand.

She took me home for coffee
I really wanted to know
She took me home for bed
'Cos I'd nowhere to go

It was a one night stand.

We started to undress
She put her clothes away
She put them in a drawer
I was glad that I could stay

It was a one night stand.

Off came her eye-lashes
Followed by her wig
Off came her make-up
She unscrewed her left leg

It was a one night stand.

She took out her lenses
She pulled out her teeth
She put in her diaphragm
And did something underneath

It was a one night stand.

She took out her bust
She put it all away
She put it in a drawer
And I didn't want to stay

It was a one night stand.

She came so very close
And then she asked for more
So I got out of bed
And I slept in the drawer

It was a one night stand.

DEATH OF A POET

The poet
Who died ·
Writing advertising slogans,
Died, with his poems
Unpublished, unfinished, unread.
The poet
Who died
Muttering the Party line
Died, thinking about Vietnam
And the Chinese bomb.
The poet
Who died
In a fluorescent-lit room,
Died, in a plastic nightmare,
Covered in a plastic bag.
The poet
Who died
In a suburban semi-detached
Watching Independent Television,
Died,
Leaving a wife and two children,
One boy, one girl,
Who died
From radiation sickness
Following the next world war.

THE TROILET

A troilet is an eight-line rhyming poem, i.e adaaabab.
The first, fourth and seventh lines are the same;
so are the second and the eighth.

THE FIRST TO BE FIXED IN THE TOILET

Poppies are red
Pot in the stew.
Have acid instead
Poppies are red;
The horse is dead
And French blues are blue:
Poppies are red
Pot in the stew.

THE SECOND TO BE READ IN THE TOILET

Let's go to bed
Yes I love you.
That's what I said
Let's go to bed;
Cos your knickers are red
And your period's not due:
Let's go to bed
Yes I love you.

RORSCHACH

SCHIZO

PHRENIC

PSYCHOPATH

MANIC,

DEPRESSIVE

When it was first published,
The Revolutionary received
widespread acclaim, and the
following are some of the numerous
press comments:—

"In The Revolutionary & Other
Poems, Stephen Morris has concocted
some diverting word designs, some
of them genuinely erotic . . ."
(The Times Higher Educational
Supplement)

"Stephen Morris is capable of
recording accurately, and touchingly,
almost naively, some small incident
of significance" (Morning Star)

"A series of clear, straightforward
poems and word pictures"
(Time Out)

"The author here is a poet/painter
and this piece of work is a fusion of
both his disciplines" (The Journal)

Some recent titles, and a selection from our back-list . . . .

The Revolutionary by Stephen Morris   cased   £1.50

second edition (paper only) revised & enlarged   50p

To Kindle The Starling by Michael Edwards

paper   £0.40

The Kingfisher Catcher by Stephen Morris

cased   £1.75

paper   £0.75

The Dark Convoys by Bryn Griffiths   cased   £1.75

paper   £0.75

Images of Stone by Bryan Walters   cased   £1.75

paper   £0.75

Prospice Vol. 1 Ed. J.C.R. Green/Michael Edwards/
Martin Booth *an anthology of new poetry, essays,
translations and review.*   paper   £0.50

cased   £1.50

Prospice Vol. 2 Ed. J.C.R. Green/Michael Edwards/
Martin Booth   paper   £0.75

cased   £1.50

**French Poetry Now (Prospice Vol. 3)
Ed Michael Edwards**   paper   £1.00

cased   £2.00

The Book of Numbers by Nick Toczek   pamphlet £0.25

Poems for Shortie by Pete Morgan   pamphlet £0.25

Prayers by George MacBeth   pamphlet £0.20

Nightride by Nicki Jackowska   pamphlet £0.20

Pilgrims & Petitions by Martin Booth   pamphlet £0.20

By Weight of Reason by J.C.R. Green   pamphlet £0.25

*for further details of these, and our other books, please
contact our distributors:*

*Aquila/IBD, 11 Novi Lane, Leek, Staffs ST13 6NS
Caveman Press, P.O. Box 1458, Dunedin, New Zealand. (inc. Australia)*
order from your bookseller, or, in case of difficulty, from
ORIEL BOOKSHOP, 53 Charles Street, Cardiff CF1 4ED.
(add 5p per title P&P)